Table of Contents

Preface

Quote is a group of words said by someone that precisely expresses what we know, recognize, feel, believe, think, accept, imagine, hope, fear, desire, acknowledge, and/or have experienced.

Quotes are motivating, inspiring, uplifting and make you think deeper, live smarter, and be extraordinary.

Additionally, quotes convey powerful emotions that help us and express our feelings, thoughts and different situations in life.

In this book, I have put together intelligent quotes of all time. Some are from famous people and some from ordinary people that said (and did) extraordinary things.

LIFE

Live your life for you, not for anyone else. Don't let the fear of being judged, rejected or disliked stop you from being yourself. – Sonya Parker.

Life is only what we choose to make it. –Michael Bradley.

Life is short. Focus from this day forward on making a difference. - Anonymous.

Life is built of the things we do. The only constructive materials are positive actions. – Anonymous.

Life is a succession of lessons which must be lived to be understood. – Helen Keller.

A life spent making mistakes is not only more honourable, but more useful than a life spent doing nothing. – George Bernard Shaw.

In life, those that are great are those that dare to follow their dreams through the good times and the bad times. – Aaliyah.

Life is change; growth is optional. Choose wisely. – Karen Kaiser Clark.

Living itself is a risky business. If we spent half as much time learning how to take risks as we spend avoiding them, we wouldn't have so much fear in life.– E. Paul Torrance.

Embrace life, have confidence in yourself, take action. – Anonymous.

The state of your life is nothing more than a reflection of your state of mind. – Dr. Wayne W. Dyer.

A great pleasure in life is doing what people say you cannot do. - Walter Gagehot.

Life is filled with possibilities. – Anonymous.

The greatest glory in living lies not in never falling, but in rising every time we fall. – Nelson Mandela.

Life is an adventure! Live it while you can. You can never have today again, tomorrow only comes once, and yesterday is gone forever. Make your choice wisely, then live the adventure you create. – Anonymous.

Life without risk is not worth living. – Charles Lindbergh.

Life is too short to ponder the "what if's" and fear rejection. – T. Dufek.

Live life with a fire that can never be extinguished. – Anonymous.

Live everyday fully as if it were your last. – Buddha.

Life is either a daring adventure or nothing at all. – Helen Keller.

Nothing can add more power to your life than concentrating all of your energies on united set of targets. – Nido Qubein.

Our lives are not determined by what happens to us, but how we react to what happens; not what life brings to us, but the attitude that we bring to life. A positive attitude causes a chain reaction of positive thoughts, events and outcomes. It is a catalyst ….a spark that creates extraordinary results. – Wade Boggs.

The game of life is to come up a winner, to be a success, and to achieve what you set out to do. – Richard Nixon.

There are two things to aim at in life; first, to get what you want and second is to enjoy it. Only the wisest of mankind achieve the second. – Logan Pearsall Smith.

Life is the most difficult exam. Many people fail because they try to copy others, not realizing that each person has a different question paper. – Anonymous.

Life is like riding a bicycle. To keep your balance you must keep moving. – Albert Einstein.

Life's challenges are not supposed to paralyze you, they are supposed to help you discover who you are. – Bernice Johnson Reagon.

Sometimes life may seem like a tunnel, endless and dark, but don't concentrate on the darkness. Concentrate on the light at the end, and you will succeed. – Julia M.

Life is a pool of risks, to live is to fight and it is even more risk to be afraid of risks. – Anonymous.

There are two ways to live your life; one is believing that nothing is a miracle, and the other is believing that everything is a miracle. – Albert Einstein.

Life is a journey with problems to solve, lessons to learn but most of all, experiences to enjoy. – Ritu Ghatourey.

I believe that everything happens for a reason. People change so that you can learn to let go, things go wrong so that you appreciate them when they are right, you believe lies so you eventually learn to trust no one but yourself, and sometimes good things fall apart so better things can fall together. – Marilyn Monroe.

Let others lead small lives, but not you. Let others argue over small things, but not you. Let others cry over small hurts, but not you. Let others leave their future in someone else's hands, but not you. – Jim Rohn.

OBSTACLES, FAILURE & SUCCESS

To win, you have to risk loss. - Jean Claude Killy.

I haven't failed; I have just found 10,000 ways that didn't work. - Thomas A. Edison.

The word 'can't' is not in the successful men's vocabulary – Anonymous.

For everything you have missed, you gained something else, and for everything you gain; you lose something else. – Walder Emerson.

Commit yourself to a dream. Nobody who tries to do something great, but fails, is a total failure. Why? Because he can always be assured that he succeeded in life's most important battle; he defeated the battle of not trying. – Robert H. Schuller.

The highest form of success …. comes…. to the man who does not shrink from danger, from hardship or from bitter toil and who out of these wins the splendid ultimate triumph. – Theodore Roosevelt.

Do you want to be a winner? Compete against yourself not somebody else. - Richard Halverson.

One's best success comes after their greatest disappointments. - Henry Ward Beeche.

What doesn't kill us makes us stronger, - Friendrich Nietzsche.

Remember that sometimes not getting what you want is a wonderful stroke of luck. – Dalai Lama.

We are all faced with a series of great opportunities brilliantly disguised as impossible situations. – Charles Swindoll.

If you learn from a loss you have not lost. – Austin O' Malley.

You can only grow if you are willing to feel awkward and uncomfortable when you try something new. - Brian Tracy.

Defeat doesn't finish a man but quit does. -Richard Nixon.

Victory is always possible for the person who refuses to stop fighting. – Napolean Hill.

Successful people tend to become more successful because they are always thinking about their successes. – Brian Tracy.

I have tried 99 times and have failed, but on the 100th time came success. – Albert Einstein.

In every problem there is a hidden treasure inside. It's your job to find it. – Asiru.

Anyone who has never made a mistake has never tried anything new. -Albert Einstein.

You may be disappointed if you fail, but you are doomed if you do not try. – Beverly Sills.

Success is the prize for those who stand true to their ideas. – John S. Hinds.

I know the price of success: dedication, hard work, and an unremitting devotion to the things you want to see happen. – Frank Lloyd Wright.

Success comes to those who dare to begin. – Gargi Nandi.

I have failed over and over again. That is why I succeed. – Michael Jordan.

Failure is merely part of the process necessary for success. – Asiru.

There are not failures in life, only those who give up too soon. – Anonymous.

He who conquers others is strong. He who conquers himself is mighty. – Lao Tzu.

Success in the end erases all the mistakes along the way. – Asiru.

To conquer without risk is to triumph without glory. – El Cid.

You miss 100% of the shots you don't take. – Wayne Gretzky.

No man ever became great without many and great mistakes. – William E. Gladstone.

There is no shortcut. Victory lies in overcoming obstacles everyday. – Asiru.

Success seems to be connected with action. Successful men keep moving; they make mistakes, but they do not quit. – Conrad Hilton.

To succeed, you need to take that gut feeling in what you believe and act on it with all of your heart. – Christy Borgeld.

Success is not where you are in life, but the obstacles you have overcome. – Booker T. Washington.

You must learn from your past mistakes, but not lean on your past successes. – Denis Waitley.

Success never comes to look for you while you wait around. You have got to get up and work at it to make your dreams come true. – Yu Khing.

Success is committing to give your best no matter what the circumstances. – Anonymous.

Success comes from having dreams that are bigger than your fears. – Terry Litwiller.

The only difference between success and failure is the ability to take action. – Alexander Graham Bell.

Real success is not having things, but having victory over yourself. – Michael.

Failure is never as scary as regret. – Anonymous.

If your life is free of failure, you are not taking enough risks. – H. Jackson Brown.

Every failure is a step to success. – William Whewell.

The men who succeed are the efficient few; they are the few who have the ambition and will power to develop themselves. – Herbert N. Casson.

Most of our obstacles would melt away if, instead of cowering before them, we should make up our minds to walk boldly through them. – Orison Swett Marden

For every problem there is an opportunity. – Robert Kiyosaki.

Failure is good. It is a fertilizer, everything I have learned about coaching I have learned from making mistakes. – Rick Petino.

Many people dream of successes. To me success can only be achieved through repeated failure and introspection. – Soichiro Honda.

Strength does not come from winning. Your struggles develop your strength. When you go through hardship and decide not to surrender, that is strength. – Arnold Schwarzenegger.

Success is not the position you stand but the direction in which you look. – Oliver Wendell Holmes.

Don't let your success of today lay you into complacency for tomorrow. For that is the worst form of failure. – Og Mandino.

In the middle of difficulty lies opportunity. – Albert Einstein.

If you want to double your success rate, you need to double your failure rate. – Thomas John Watson, Sr.

In every problem there is opportunity to win or lose, rise or fall... Your actions or reactions are the deciding factor. – I. Joseph.

Relentlessness and discontent are the first necessities of progress. – Thomas A. Edison.

Believe and act as if it were impossible to fail. – Charles Kettering.

You cannot have any success unless you can accept failure. – Dell Crossword.

The harder you fall, the higher you bounce. – Dong Horton.

Success is determined by those who prove the impossible to be possible. – James W. Pence.

The only real failure is the one from which we learn nothing. – John Powell.

Success is not the key to happiness, Happiness is not the key to success. If you love what you are doing, you will be successful. – Herman Cain.

In order to succeed you must fail, so you know what to do better the next time. - Anthony D. Angelo.

Success is a state of mind. If you want success, start thinking of yourself as a success. - Dr. Joyce Brothers.

Each problem has in it an opportunity so powerful that it literally dwarfs the problem. The greatest success stories were created by people who recognized a problem and turned it into an opportunity. - Joseph Sugarman.

I never expect to lose. Even when I am the underdog, I still prepare a victory speech. - H. Jackson Browne.

Success doesn't come to you; you go to it. – Marva Collins.

I have missed more than 9,000 shots in my career. I have lost almost 300 games. On 26 occasions, I have been entrusted to take the game winning shots ..... and I missed, I have failed over and over and over again in my life and that's precisely why I succeed. – Michael Jordan.

It takes time to succeed because to succeed is merely the natural reward of taking time to do anything well. – Joseph Ross.

A man is a success if he gets up in the morning and goes to bed at night, and in between does what he wants to do. - Bob Dylan.

Men are born to succeed, not fail. - Henry David Thoreau.

Whenever I hear it can't be done, I know I am close to success. – Michael Flatley.

Success is to go from one failure to another with no loss of enthusiasm. - Winston Churchill.

Most success springs from an obstacle or failure – Scott Adams.

The truth is that all of us can attain the greatest success and happiness possible in this life whenever we use our native capacities to their greatest extent. – Smiley Blanton.

The first and most important step toward success is the feeling that we can succeed. – Nelson Boswell.

I don't know the key to success, but the key to failure is trying to please everybody. – Bill Cosby.

The secret to success in life is for a man to be ready for his opportunity when it comes. – Benjamin Disraeli.

It is only as we develop others we permanently succeed.- Harvey Samuel Firestone.

Successful people do what unsuccessful people dare not to. – Jim Rohn.

Coming together is the beginning, keeping together is progress, working together is success. – Henry Ford.

The most absurd and reckless aspirations have sometimes led to extraordinary success. – Luc de Clapiers.

Losers visualize the penalties of failure, winners visualize the rewards of success. – William S. Gilbert.

Of course we all have our limits, but how can you possibly find your boundaries unless you explore as far and as wide as you possibly can? I would rather fail at an attempt at something new and unchartered, than safely succeed in a repeat of something I have already done. - A.E Hotchner.

The road to success is always under construction. – Lily Tomlin.

None of the secrets of success will work unless you do. – Anonymous.

Success comes in can's. failure comes in can't. – Michael Josephson.

There are no speed limits on the road to success. – David W. Johnson.

Character cannot be developed in ease and quiet. Only through experience, trial, and suffering can the soul be strengthened, vision cleared, ambition inspired, and success achieved. – Helen Keller.

There is no great success without great commitment. – Anthony Robbins.

Many a man has finally succeeded only because he has failed after repeated efforts. If he had never met defeat, he would never have known any great victory. – Orison Swett Marden.

If you want to be successful, it's just this simple: know what you are doing, love what you are doing, and believe in what you are doing. – Will Rogers

The only thing ever achieved in life without effort is failure. – Francis of Assisi.

It is far better to dare mighty things to win glorious triumphs, even though checkered with failure, than to make rank with those poor spirits who neither enjoy much nor suffer much, because they are in the grey twilight that knows not victory or defeat. – Theodore Roosevelt.

Men succeed when they realize that their failures are the preparation for their victories. - Ralph Waldo Emerson.

Success consists of getting up just one more time than you fall. - Oliver Goldsmith.

Success is doing what you want to do, when you want, with whomever you want, as much as you want. – Anthony Robbins.

Past failures are guidepost for future success. – Anonymous.

Even a mistake may turn out to be the one thing necessary to a worthwhile achievement. – Henry Ford.

When defeat comes, accept it as a signal that your plans are not sound. Rebuild those plans and set sail once more toward your coveted goal. – Napolean Hill.

I have learned that we cannot forget or throw away our past, but we must not let our past to control us either, we must learn and grow from our past failures, disappointments, and painful experiences, reset our goals and priorities and move forward, start today by untying the knots that are limiting you. – Ty Howard.

If you want to be successful, find someone who has achieved the results you want, and copy what they do, and you'll achieve similar results. – Anthony Robbins.

Success is achieved and maintained by those who try, and keep trying, for there is nothing to lose by trying and a great deal to gain if successful. By all means try! Do it NOW. – W. Clement Stone.

Use failures as stepping – stones to deeper understanding and greater achievement. – Susan Taylor.

The real risk is doing nothing. - Denis Waitley.

Plan to succeed or you have planned to fail. – Benjamin Franklin.

Great people are created by great mistakes that are learned from, not from great successes that are gloated upon. - Elmer Clark.

Those who want to succeed will find a way; those who don't will find an excuse. – Leo Aguila.

If you mess up and learn nothing, it's a mistake. If you mess up and learn something; it's an experience. – Mark Mcfadden.

People who are afraid to fail can never experience the joys of success. – J.K. Rowling.

Impossibility is an opinion, not a fact. – Anonymous.

The surest way not to fail is to be determined to succeed. – Richard Brinsley Sheridan.

True success is the overcoming the fear of being unsuccessful. – Paul Sweeney.

If at first you don't succeed, dust yourself off and try again. – Aaliyah.

Some of the best lessons we ever learn are learned from past mistakes. The error of the past is the wisdom and success of the future. - Dr. Dale Turner.

Some people succeed because they are destined to, but most people succeed because they are determined to. – Henry Van Dyke.

To be a winner, all you have to give is all you have. – Asiru.

Don't limit your challenges, challenge your limits. – Jerry Dunn.

Happiness is the highest level of success. – Asiru.

He who dares, wins. – Winston Churchill.

Only those who risk going too far can possibly find out how far one can go. - T.S Eliot.

It's not whether you get knocked down; it's whether you get back up. – Vince Lombardi.

The door to success is the one marked PUSH. – Anonymous.

Winners are ordinary people with extraordinary heart. – Anonymous.

Keys to success: research your ideas, plan for success, expect success, and just do it. - John S. Hinds.

I am not judged by the number of times I fail, but the number of times I succeed, and the number of times I succeed is a direct proportion to the number of times I fail and keep trying. - Tom Hopkins.

Do not settle for less than an extraordinary life. – Anonymous.

Out of difficulties grow miracles. - Jean De La Bruyere.

To be successful you must decide exactly what you want to accomplish, and then resolve to pay the price to get it. - Bunker Hunt.

We cannot discover new oceans until we have the courage to lose sight of the shore. - Andre Gide.

There is only one way to fail and that is to quit. – Anonymous.

It is no sin to attempt and fail. The only sin is to not make the attempt. - Swellen Fried.

The law of cause and effect; if you do what other successful people do, you will eventually get the results that other successful people get. - Brian Tracy.

If you have failed, do not worry. You have just cut the way to success.   - Anonymous.

Excellence is attained when you care more than others think is wise, risk more than others think is safe; dream more than others think is practical; expect more than others think is possible. -Jim Gentil.

Success could be described as 50/50 – 50% vision and 50% action. – Anonymous.

The man who can drive himself farther once the effort gets painful is the man who will win. - Roger Bannister.

Every worthwhile accomplishment, big or little, has its stages of drudgery and triumph, a beginning, a struggle, and a victory. – Ghandi.

Never confuse a single defeat with a final defeat. - F. Scott Fitzgerald.

There is no failure only feedback. - Robert Allen.

Failure is a success if we learn from it. - Malcolm Forbes.

Only those who dare to fail greatly can ever achieve greatly. - Robert Francis Kennedy

Winning starts with beginning. – Robert H. Schuller.

It still holds true that man is most uniquely human when he turns obstacles into opportunities. - Eric Hoffer.

Challenge yourself all the days of your life. - Anonymous.

Unless you are willing to try, fail miserably and try again, success won't happen. - Phillip Adams.

The will to win, the desire to succeed, the urge to reach your full potential. These are the keys that will unlock the door to personal excellence. - Eddie Robinson.

Seek not outside yourself for success lies within. - Mary Lou Cook.

Every great achievement was once considered impossible. – H. Jackson Brown.

Difficulties mastered are opportunities won.-Winston Churchill.

Success depends upon our previous preparations, and without such preparations there is sure to be failure. – Confucious.

Stumbling is not the same as falling. –Malcolm X.

The greater the obstacle, the more glory in achieving it. –Moliere.

Assert your right to make a few mistakes and learn from them. Mistakes are the lessons of wisdom. - Anonymous.

Nothing will come of nothing; we must dare mighty things.- William Shakespeare.

History has demonstrated that the most notable winners usually encountered heartbreaking obstacles before they succeeded. They won because they refused to become discouraged by their defeat. - B.C Forbes.

If anyone else can do it, or make it in life, so can I. - Thomas J. Vilord.

You can't hit a home run unless you step up to the plate. You can't catch a fish if you don't put your line in the water. You can't reach your goals if you don't try. - Kathy Seligman.

Go as far as you can see and when you get there you will see further. - Orison Swett Marden.

No one knows what he can do until he tries. - Publilius Syrus.

Success is willing to do what the unsuccessful person is not willing to do. – Jeff Olson.

Keep on trying…. each failure is one step closer to a success. -Thomas J. Vilord.

Success is not final and failure is not fatal. It is the courage to continue that counts. - Winston CHurchill.

Before success comes in any man's life, he is sure to meet with much temporary defeats, and perhaps some failures. When defeat overtakes a man, the easiest and most logical to do is to quit. That is what the majority of men do. That is why the majority is just ordinary. - Napoleon Hill.

Unless you have tried to do something beyond what you have already mastered, you will never grow. - Ronald E. Osborn.

Forget past mistakes and forget failures. Forget everything except what you are going to do now and do it. - William Durant.

There is only one success – to be able to spend your life in your own way that you want. - Christopher Morley.

Aim for success, not perfection. Never give up your right to be wrong, because then you will lose your ability to learn new things and move forward in your life. - Dr. David M.

You always pass failure on the way to success.- Mickey Rooney.

You cannot have everything, but you can try.- Anonymous.

A minute of success pays for years of failure.- Robert Browning.

Never let your failures go to you heart or your successes go to your head. – Soichiro Honda.

Failure is instructive. The person who really thinks, learns just as much from his failures as he does from his successes. - John Dewey.

There is no point at which you can say, "well I am successful now, I might as well relax". - Carrie Fisher.

Champions know that success is inevitable, that there is no such thing as failure, only feedback. They know that the best way to forecast the future is to create it.- Michale J. Gelb.

It is the man who has done nothing that says nothing can be done. – Anonymous.

The men who try to do something and fail are infinitely better than those who do nothing and succeed. -Lloyd Jones.

An inventor fails 999 times, and if he succeeds once, he is victorious. He treats his failures as practice shoots. - Charles Franklin Kettering.

A powerful combination to ensure success is having the vision of an eagle and the heart of a lion. –Robert G. Allen.

I wasn't afraid to fail. Something good always comes out of failure.- Anne Baxter.

The difference between a successful person and the others is not a lack of strength and not a lack of knowledge, but a lack of will. -Vince Lombardi.

An obstacle may be either a stepping-stone or a stumbling block. – Anonymous.

Failing to plan is planning to fail.-Effie Jones.

There are no secrets to success. It is the result of preparation, hard work, and learning from failure. - Colin Powell.

Never mind what others do; do better than yourself, beat your own record each day and everyday and you are a success. - William Boetcker.

There are two ways of meeting difficulties. You can alter the difficulties, or you can alter yourself to meet the difficulties. - Phyllis Bottoms.

To succeed, it is necessary to accept the world as it is and rise above it. - Michael Korda.

Failure is simply an opportunity to begin again ….. This time more intelligently. - Henry Ford.

The recipe of success is to study while others are sleeping, work while others are loafing, prepare while others are playing, and dream while others are wishing. - William A. Ward.

The successful man will profit from his mistakes and try again in a different way. - Dale Carnegie.

Some of my fondest memories in sports were a result of failures, injuries, setbacks, and mistakes. I learned far more about myself and gained more character in those difficult times than I ever did when success came early. - Peter Vidmar.

A bump in the road is either an obstacle to be fought, or an opportunity to be enjoyed.- Anonymous.

Out of respect of things I was never destined to do, I have learned that my strengths are a result of my weakness, my success is due to my failures, and my style is directly related to my limitations. - Billy Joel.

You must think of failure and defeat as the spring boards to new achievements, and to the next level of accomplishment.- Les Brown.

The secret to success is to do common things uncommonly well.- John D. Rockefeller, Sr.

Nothing stops a man who desires to achieve. Every obstacle is simply a course to develop his achievement muscles, it's a strengthening of his powers toward accomplishment.- Eric Butterworth.

He has achieved success if he has lived well, laughed often, and loved much. – Bessie Stanley.

In adversity keep motivated, because often the best result comes from difficulties. – Norman Vincent Peale.

Never use the word "impossible". Throw it into the verbal waste bucket. – Jacki French.

Success is directly proportional to effort. – Anonymous.

There are risks and costs to a plan of action, but they are far less than the long-term risks and costs of comfortable inactions. – John F. Kennedy.

When facing a difficult task, act as if you cannot fail. – H. Jackson Brown.

One of the most important principle of success is developing the habit of going the extra mile. - Napolean Hill.

A winner never stops trying. – Tom Landry.

Success is having your best day every day. – Anonymous.

Winners must have two things; definite goal and a burning desire to achieve them. – Brad Burden.

The three P's of success: passion, persistence, and patience. – Dong Bronson.

If you are successful, you may win false friends and true enemies. Succeed anyway. – Mother Theresa.

Yesterday's failures are today's seeds that must be diligently planted to be able to abundantly harvest tomorrow's success. – Anonymous.

Forget about the consequences of failure. Failure is only a temporary change in direction to set you straight for your next success. – Denis Waitley.

There is a gift in every hardship. – Anonymous.

No one makes a lock without a key, that's why God won't give you problems without solutions. – Oliver Wendell Holmes.

I can accept failure, everyone fails at something. But I can't accept not trying. – Michael Jordan.

Nothing is permanent in this wicked world not even our troubles. – Charlie Chaplin.

Opportunity is missed by most because it is dressed in overalls and looks like work. – Thomas Edison.

Never give up! Failure and rejection are only the first step to succeeding. – Jimmy Valvano.

Shoot for the moon. If you fall short at least you'll be among the stars. – Les Brown.

Take a risk – Jump out of your comfort zone. – Harvey Mackey.

Take up one idea and act on it. Make that one idea your life. Think of it, dream of it, and live on that idea. Let the brain, muscles, nerves, and every part of your body be full of that idea and leave all other ideas alone. This is the way to success. – Swami Vivekananda.

The ultimate measure of a man is not where he stands in moments of comfort and convenience, but where he stands at times of challenges and controversy. – Dr. Martin Luther King, J.

Opportunities are usually disguised as hard work, so most people don't recognize them. – Ann Landers.

Every great work, every great accomplishment, has been brought into manifestation through holding to the vision, and often comes apparent and temporary failure and discouragement just before the big achievement. – Florence Scove Shinn.

You have to find something that you love enough to be able to take risks, jump over the hurdles and break through the brick walls that are always going to be placed in front of you. If you don't have that kind of feeling for what it is you are doing, you'll stop at the first giant hurdle. – George Lucas.

On the path to success, always lies big O's. Some read them as Obstacle, and others read them as Opportunities. – Poh Yu Khing.

I feel the most important requirement to success is learning how to overcome failure. You must learn to tolerate it, but never accept it. – Reggie Jackson.

The secret of success is learning how to use pain and pleasure instead of having pain and pleasure use you. If you do that, you are in control of your life. If you don't, life controls you. – Anthony Robbins.

Entrepreneurs are simply those who understand that there is little difference between obstacle and opportunity, and are able to turn both to their advantage. – Victor Kiam.

FOCUS – Follow One Course Until Successful. – Robert Kiyosaki.

Your ego can become an obstacle to your work. If you start believing in your greatness, it is the death of your creativity. – Marina Abramovic.

FEAR, COURAGE & CONFIDENCE

The secret of happiness is freedom. The secret of freedom is courage. – Thucydides.

Never let your fears be the boundaries of your dreams. - Anonymous.

Innovate, develop, motivate, inspire, trust – be a leader. – Anonymous.

Worry is a waste of time. Worry clogs the brain and paralyzes the thought. A troubled brain cannot think clearly, vigorously and wisely.– Orison Swett Marden.

Brain cells create ideas, stress kills brain cells. – Frederick Saunders.

Consult not your fears, but your hopes and your dreams. Think not about your frustrations, but about your unfulfilled potentials. Concern yourself not with what you have tried and failed in, but with what it is still possible for you to do. – Pope John XXIII.

All of our dreams can come true if we have the courage to pursue them. – Walt Disney.

Experience tells you what to do. Confidence allows you to do it. – Stan Smith.

Overcome fear by taking action. – Anonymous.

Courage is not the absence of fear, but rather the judgment that something else is more important than one's fear. – Ambrose Redmoon.

What is fear? F=false, E= evidence, A=appearing, R= real. Don't be afraid of only false evidence, just do it. – Anonymous.

The history of the human race is the history of ordinary people who have overcome their fears and have accomplished extraordinary things. – Brian Tracy.

If one advances confidently in the direction of his own dreams and endeavours to live the life that he has imagined, he will meet with a success unexpected in common hours. – Henry David Thoreau.

Courage changes things for the better. With courage, you can stay with something long enough to succeed at it, realizing that it usually takes two, three, or four times as long to succeed as you thought or hoped. – Earl Nightingale.

Courage is daring to take the first step, or a different path. It is the decision to place your dreams above your fears. – Anonymous.

What you can do, or dream you can, begin it. Boldness has genius, power, and magic in it. – Johann Wolfgang von Goethe.

Fear is met and destroyed with courage. Again and again when the struggle seems hopeless and all opportunity lost, the one with a little more courage and a little more effort will have victory. – James F. Bell.

Don't be afraid to go after what you want to do and what you want to be, and don't be afraid to pay the price to get it. – Anonymous.

Be courageous! Have faith! Go forward. -Thomas A. Edison.
Everything you want is on the other side of fear. – Jack Cornfield.

Fear begins to melt away when you begin to take action on a goal you really want. – Robert G. Allen.

Great work is done by people who are not afraid to be great. – Fernando Plores.

The greatest mistake you can make in your life is to be continually fearing that you will make one. – Elbert Hubbard.

Whenever you see a successful business, someone once made courageous decision. – Peter Drucker.

The highest courage is to dare to be yourself in the face of adversity. Choosing right over wrong, ethics over convenience, and truth over popularity. These are the choices that measure your life. Travel the path of integrity without looking back, for there will never be a wrong time to do the right thing. – Michael Moore.

One can choose to go back toward safety or forward toward growth. Growth must be chosen again and again; fear must be overcome again and again. – Abraham Maslow.

We must have courage to bet on our ideas, take the calculated risk, and take action. – Martin Brown.

The fear you let build in your mind is worse than the situation that really exist. – Spencer Johnson.

Don't let self-doubt and criticism hold you back. – William Bentley.

Choose your dreams and leave your doubts behind. – Chris Scott.

I spent twelve years working with cattle; yet I never saw a Jersey cow running a temperature because the pasture was burning from lack of rain or because of sleet and cold or because her boyfriend was paying too much attention to another heffer. The animals confront night, storms and hunger calmly; so they never have nervous breakdowns or stomach ulcers; and they never go insane. – Dale Carnegie.

Everyone admires the bold, no one honours the timid. – Robert Greene.

Timidity is dangerous; better to enter with boldness. – Robert Greene.
A day of worry is more exhausting than a week of work. - L. John.

Expect to succeed even before you start. All winners, no matter what their game, start with the expectations that they are going to succeed. Winners say, "I want to do this and I CAN do this", not " I would like to do this, but I don't think I can." - Denis Waitley.

Aim for the top, for there is plenty of rooms up there. There are so few at the top, it is almost lonely there. – Samuel Insull.

Everyone has a fair turn to be as great as he pleases. – Jeremy Collier

The most important thing is to know that you can do it. – Robert G. Allen.

The one thing worse than a quitter is the person who is afraid to begin. – Anonymous.

All of our dreams can come true if we have the courage to pursue them. – Walt Disney.

Nothing great was ever achieved without risk. No risk no reward. – Anonymous.

The key to winning is self confidence and the key to self confidence is preparation. – Arthur Arshe.

Courage is the greatest of all virtues, because if you haven't courage, you may not have an opportunity to use any of the others. – Samuel Johson.

Success is never final, failure is never fatal. It's courage that counts. – John Wooden.

One man with courage is a majority. – Thomas Jefferson.

Life begins where fear ends. – Osho.

A man full of courage is also full of faith. – Cicero.

Courage is resistance to fear, mastery of fear, not absence of fear. – Mark Twain.

Clear thinking requires courage rather than intelligence. – Thomas Szasz.

Life shrinks or expands in proportion to one's courage. – Anais Nin.

The biggest obstacle to wealth is fear. People are afraid to think big, but if you think small, you'll only achieve small things. – T. Harv Eker.

GOALS, HARD – WORK & CHANGE

If you can't change the circumstances, change your perspective. - Anonymous.

Thriving for success without hard work is like trying to harvest where you haven't planted. – David Bly.

Cause change and lead; accept change and survive; resist change and die. – Ray Norda.

The achievement of one goal should be the starting point of another. – Alexander Graham Bell.

The only difference between dreams and achievements is hardwork. – Major Chris Bollwage.

In the long run, we only hit what we aim at. – Henry David Thoreau.
There are no limitations to any of our dreams. – Gene Simmons.

Focus on where you want to go, not where you currently are. – Anonymous.

You can turn negative consequences into positive rewards simply by changing your habits now. – Mark Victor Hansen.

Do not let what you cannot do interfere with what you can do. – John Wooden.

If you have goals and procrastination you have nothing. If you have goals and you take action, you will have anything you want. – Thomas J. Vilord.

Remember, if you want a different result, do something different. – Anonymous.

If I can dream, I can act and if I can act, I can become. – Poh Yu khing.

Hope doesn't guarantee anything but hardwork does. – Anonymous.

Spectacular achievement is always preceded by painstaking preparation. – Roger Staubach.

 If we did all of the things we are capable of doing, we would literally surprise ourselves. – Thomas A. Edison.

Plan your work for today and everyday and then work on your plan today and everyday. – Norman Vincent Peale.

The only place success comes before work is in the dictionary. – Donald Kendall.

If what you did yesterday seems big, you haven't done anything today. – Lou Holtz.

Your dreams come true when you act to turn them into realities.- Anonymous.

You don't have to be a fantastic hero to do certain things to compete. You can just be an ordinary person, sufficiently motivated to reach challenging goals. – Sir Edmund Hillary.

It had long since come to my attention that people of accomplishment rarely sat back and let things happen to them. They went out and made things happen. – Elinor Smith.

Dreams are renewable. No matter what our age or condition, there are still untapped possibilities within us, and a new beauty waiting to be born. -Dr. Dale Turner.

If you continue to work hard, success will follow you. – Anonymous.

You don't have to be great to get started, but you have to get started to be great. – Les Brown.

The harder I work, the luckier I get. – James Thurber.

Dreams are the reality of tomorrow. – Dean Marshall.

Do not go where the path may lead, go instead where there is no path and leave a trail. – Ralph Waldo Emerson.

Complaining is silly, either act or forget. – Stefan Sagmeister.

This one step, choosing a goal and sticking to it, changes everything. – Scoth Reed.

Without goals and a plan to reach them, you are like a ship that has set sail with no destination. – Fitzhugh Dodson.

A thousand mile journey begins with one step. – Lao Tsu.

You must have long-term goals to keep you from being frustrated by short-term failures. – Charles C. Noble.

You are successful the moment you start moving toward a worthwhile goal.– Charles Carlson.

Goals that are not written down are just wishes. – Fitzhugh Dodson.
Let your heart soar as high as it will. Refuse to be average.   –A.W Tozer.

The more goals you set, the more goals you get. – Mark Victor Hansen.

I like the dreams of the future better than the history of the past. – Thomas Jefferson.

The more you prospect the more you prosper. – Steve Johnson.

The truth of the matter is that there is nothing you can't accomplish if you clearly decide what it is that you are absolutely committed to achieving, you are willing to take massive action, and you continue to change your approach until you achieve what you want, using whatever life gives you along the way. – Anthony Robbins.

My will shall shape my future. Whether I fail or succeed shall be no man's doing but my own. I am the force; I can clear any obstacle before me, or I can be lost in a maze. My choices, my responsibility, win or lose, only I hold the key to my destiny. - Elaine Maxwell.

Without continual growth and progress, such words as improvement, achievement, and success have no meaning. – Barrack Obama.

Nothing is as real as a dream. Have the courage to reach for it. – Earl Nightingale.

Never give up on a dream just because of the time it will take to accomplish it. The time will pass anyway. – Anonymous.

Achievement comes when you decide to live your possibilities. – Anonymous.

Climb high, climb far, the sky is your goal, the star is your aim. – Inscription on steps. William Colleges.

Vision without action is merely a dream. Action without vision just passes time. Vision with action can change the world. - Joel Barker.

A person is led on the path that he truly wants to travel on. - Talmud.

You can change all things for the better when you change yourself for the better. –Jim Rohn.

One must have strategies to execute his dreams. – Azim Premji.

Working hard overcomes a whole lot of other obstacles. You can have unbelievable intelligence, you can have connections, and you can have opportunities fall out of the sky. But in the end, hard work is the true, enduring characteristic of successful people. - Marsha Evans.

If you have talent and you work long and hard at it, anything in the world can be yours. – Anonymous.

Just like a turtle, we only make progress if we stick our neck out. – James Bryant Conant.

Start by doing what is necessary, then what is possible, and suddenly you are doing the impossible. – Francis of Assisi.

Goals are like the stars; they are always there. Adversity is like clouds: they are temporary and will move on, keep your eyes on the stars. – Byrd Baggett.

Leaders are not born; they are made. And they are made just like anything else-through hard work, and that is the price we'll have to pay to achieve any goal. – Vince Lombardi.

Discipline is the bridge between goal and accomplishment. – Jim Rohn.

Successful men and women are big dreamers. They imagine what their future could be, ideal in every respect, and then they work everyday toward their distant vision, goal, and purpose. – Brian Tracy.

If we don't change, we don't grow. If we don't grow, we are not really living. – Gail Sheehy.

If you can dream it, you can do it. Your limits are all within yourself. – Brian Tracy.

Society may predicts, but only I can determine my destiny. – Clair Oliver.

If we are to achieve results never before accomplished, we must expect to employ methods never before attempted. – Francis Bacon.

People with goals succeed because they know where they are going. – Earl Nightingale.

If you have a burning desire and a plan to take action, there is absolutely nothing you cannot achieve. – Thomas J. Vilord.

God created all men equal. Why do some accomplish far greater accomplishments than others? Because they had a vision, a desire, and they took action. – Thomas J. Vilord.

The starting point of all achievements is desire. Keep this constantly in mind. Weak desire brings weak results, just as a small amount of fire makes a small amount of heat. – Napoleon Hill.

If we always look back, we lose sight of what is ahead. – Justin Sims.

Do not settle for less than an extraordinary life. – Anonymous.

Destiny is not a matter of chance, it's a matter of choice. It is not a thing to be waited for; it is a thing to be achieved. - Jeremy Kitson.

If you want your life to be a magnificent story, then begin by realizing that you are the author and everyday you have the opportunity to write a new page. – Mark Houlghan.

It is in your moments of decision that your destiny is shaped. – Anthony Robbins.

It's so hard when contemplated in advance and so easy when you just do it. – Robert M. Pirsig.

The one thing that separates the winners from the losers, is, winners take action. – Anthony Robins.

It is not what you say or hope, wish or intend, but only what you do that counts. Your choices tell you unerringly who you really are. – Brian Tracy.

A time comes when you need to stop waiting for the man you want to become and start being the man you want to be. – Bruce Springsteen.

You are what you repeatedly do. Excellence is not an event. – it is a habit. – Aristotle.

Things do not change, we change. – Henry David Thoreau.

Hold yourself to a higher standard than anybody else expects of you. – Henry Ward Beecher.

To move the world, we must first move ourselves. – Socrates.

If you do what you have always done, you get what you have always gotten.
- Anthony Robbins.

The world makes way for a man who knows where he is going.-Ralph Waldo Emerson.

He who stops being better, stops being good. -Oliver Cromwell.

It is good to dream, but it is better to dream and work. Faith is mighty, but faith with action is mightier. Desiring is helpful, but desire and work is invincible. – Thomas Robert Gaines.

Don't be afraid of the space between your dreams and reality. If you can dream it, you can make it so. – Belva Davis.

If you want your dreams to come true then WAKE UP! – J.M. Power.

Everything changes when you change. – Jim Rohn.

A person with a clear purpose will make progress on even the roughest road. A person with no purpose will make no progress even on the smoothest road. – Thomas Carlyle.

You can't hit a target you cannot see and you cannot see a target you do not have. – Zig Ziglar.

Joy is when anticipation meets action. – Anonymous.

Always look at what you have left and what is left to come. Never look at what you have lost. - Robert H. Schuler.

We cannot become what we want to be by remaining what we are. – Max Depree.

Great minds have purposes, others have wishes. Little minds are tamed and subdued by misfortunes, but great minds rise above them.– Washington Irving.

Tomorrow belongs to those who have vision today.– Robert Schuller.

The price of success is hard work, dedicated to the job at hand, and the determination that whether we win or lose, we have applied the best of ourselves to the task at hand. – Vince Lombardi.

To have more than you have got, become more than you are. – Jim Rohn.

If you want your dreams to come true, don't oversleep. – Nicky Gumbel.

We cannot change yesterday, we can only make the most of today and look with hope toward tomorrow. – Anonymous.

Cherish your visions and your dreams, as they are the children of your soul, and the blueprints of your ultimate achievement. – Napolean Hill.

Action, to be effective, must be directed to clearly conceived ends. – J. Nehru.

You can do what you want to do, accomplish what you want to accomplish, attain any reasonable objective you may have in mind, not all of a sudden, perhaps not in one swift and sweeping act of achievement, but you can do it gradually, day by day, and play by play, if you want to do it, if you work to do it, over a sufficiently long period of time. – William E. Holler.

Never give up, if you want to be something be conceited about it. Give yourself a chance. Never say that you are not good for that will never get you anywhere. Set high goals. That is what life is all about. – Mike Mclaren.

Think little goals and expect little achievements. Think big goals and win big successes. – David Joseph Schwartz.

He who labours diligently need never despair, for all things are accomplished by diligence and labour. – Menander.

The roots of true achievement lie in the will to become the best that you can become. – Herold Taylor.

No life ever grows great until it is focused, dedicated, and disciplined. – Henry Emerson Forsdick.

It takes a person who is wide – awake to make his dream come true. – Roger Ward Babson.

Work like you don't need the money, love like you have never been hurt, and dance like nobody is watching. – Mark Twain.

God puts people in your life for a reason and removes them from your life for a better reason. – Dr. Bilal Philips.

When someone leaves you don't feel lonely inside, but teach yourself how to be more independent. – Anonymous.

Some people want it to happen, some wish it would happen, others make it happen. – Michael Jordan.

The secret of success is consistency of purpose. – Benjamin Disraeli.

Decide what is worthwhile and follow through with it. – Anonymous.

Do extraordinary things; don't just dream them. – Nicolina.

There is one quality that one must posses to win, and that is definiteness of purpose, the knowledge of what one wants, and a burning desire to posses it. – Napoleon Hill.

Doing your best is more important than being the best. – Shannon Miller.

I am a great believer in luck, and I find that the harder I work the more luck I have.   – Thomas Jefferson.

Action is a great restorer and builder of confidence, inaction are not only the result, but the cause of fear. – Norman Vincent Peale.

LEARNING, BELIEF & THOUGHT

It is not the events of our lives that shape us, but our beliefs as to what those events mean. – Tony Robbins.

A man sees in the world what he carries in his heart. – Johann Wolfgang von Goethe.

We become what we think about. – Earl Nightingale.

The heart is like a garden: it can grow compassion or fear, resentment or love. What seeds will you plant there? – Jack Cornfield.

You don't need strength to let go of something. What you really need is understanding. – Guy Finley.

It is not the quantity but the quality of knowledge which determines the mind's dignity. – William Ellery Channing.

Our mind is the most valuable possession that we have. The quality of our lives is, and will be, a reflection of how well we develop, train, and utilize this precious gift. – Brian Tracy.

Approach the start of each day with something in mind and end the day with one word…. DONE. – Anonymous.

Money never starts an idea; it's the idea that starts the money. – Mark Victor Hansen.

Never stop learning. If you learn one new thing everyday, you will overcome 99% of your competition. – Joe Carlozo.

Man is what he believes. – Anton Chekov.

The day I stop giving is the day I stop receiving. The day I stop learning is the day I stop growing. You miss 100% of the shots you don't' take. – Wayne Gretzky.

Discovery lies in seeing what everyone sees, but thinking what no one has thought. – Albert Szent Gyorgyi.

You cannot always control what goes on outside, but you can control what goes on inside. – Wayne Dyer.

There are essentially two things that will make us wiser: the books we read and the people we meet. – Charles Jones.

All leaders are readers. – Jim Rohn.

Believe you will be successful and you will. - Dale Carnegie.

Nothing is possible if you think it is impossible. Nothing is impossible if you think it is possible. Think possible and work hard, and ANYTHING is possible. – Thomas J. Vilord.

Anything you vividly imagine, ardently desire, sincerely believe, and enthusiastically act upon must come to reality. – Paul J. Meyer.

It is not enough to have knowledge; one must apply it. it is not enough to have wishes; one must also accomplish them. – Johann Wolfgang von Goethe.

Become a possibilitarian. No matter how dark things seem to be or actually are, raise your sights and see the possibilities – always see them, for they are always there. – Norman Vincent Peale.

Our limitations and successes will be based most often on our own expectations for ourselves. What the mind dwells upon, the body acts upon. – Thomas Dewar.

The pessimist sees difficulty in every opportunity; an optimist sees the opportunity in every difficulty. – Winston Churchill.

You can change the way you feel by changing the way you think. – Dennis Greenberger.

I am the captain of my soul. I am the master of my fate. – William Henley.

Thought is the original source of all wealth, all success, all material gain, all great discoveries and inventions, and all achievements. – Claude M. Bristol.

The mind quickly responds to teaching and discipline. You can make the mind gives you back anything you want. – Norman Vincent Peale.

Don't think problem, think opportunity. – Anonymous.

Learn to listen. Opportunity sometimes knocks very softly. – Ronald Oliver.

Nothing can stop the man with the right mental attitude from achieving his goal; nothing on earth can help the man with wrong mental attitude. – Thomas Jefferson.

Ability is what you are capable of doing. Motivation determines what you do. Attitude determines how well you do it. – Lou Holtz.

There is no limit to what a man can achieve if he so believes this. - Thomas J. Vilord.

Trust yourself. Create the kind of person that you will be happy with all your life. Make the most of yourself by fanning the tiny inner sparks of possibility into flames of achievement. – Foster C. McClellan.

Within us are the seeds of triumph or defeat. Which seeds will you plant?. – Longfellow.

If you believe you can, then you will. Have confidence in your abilities, and then follow through with them. – Anonymous.

If you can command yourself, you can command the world. – Anonymous.

The greatest discovery is that a human being can alter his life by altering his attitudes of his mind. – William James.

As a rule, he or she that has the most information will have the greatest success in life. – Benjamin Disraeli.

To achieve, you must believe something and want something with all your might. Then you must be willing to commit yourself to a course. – Anonymous.

It is not enough to have a good mind; the important thing is to use it well. – Rene Descartes.

If there is any one axiom that I have tried to live up to in attempting to become successful in business, it is the act that I have tried to surround myself with friends that know more about business than I do. This policy has always been very successful and is still working for me. – Monte L. Bean.

If you believe you can, you probably can, if you believe you won't, you most assuredly won't. Belief is the ignition switch that gets you off the launching pad. – Denis Waitley.

Throw back the shoulders, let the heart sing, let the eyes flash, let the mind be lifted up, look upward and say to yourself, nothing is impossible!!! – Norman Vincent Peale.

You are today where your thoughts have brought you; you will be tomorrow where your thoughts take you. – James Allen.

You must do the things you think you cannot do. – Eleanor Roosevelt.

A man achieves according to what he believes. – Warren Weir.

An optimist expects his dreams to come true. A pessimist expects his nightmares to come true. – Lauren J. Peter.

The desire of knowledge, like the thirst of riches, increases ever with the acquisition of it. - Laurence Sterne.

The intelligent man is one, who has successfully fulfilled many accomplishments, and is still willing to learn more. - Ed Parker.

Ideas are the beginning of all achievements. - Bruce Lee.

Believe in yourself! Have faith in your abilities! Without a humble, but reasonable confidence in your own powers, you cannot be successful or happy. - Norman Vincent Peale.

Great things are completed by talented people who believe they will accomplish them. - Warren G. Bennis.

For a man to achieve all that is demanded of him, he must regard himself as greater than he is. - Johann Wolfgang von Goethe.

Wisdom is knowing what to do next, virtue is doing it. –David Jordan.

Every achiever that I have ever met says "My life turned around when I began to believe in me." – Robert H. Schuller.

If you think you can win, you can win. Faith is necessary for victory. – William Hazlitt.

The future belongs to those who see possibility before they become obvious. – John Sculley.

The body achieves what the mind believes. – Jim Evans.

To accomplish great things, we must not only act, but also dream, not only plan, but also believe. – Anatole France.

To be a champion, you have to believe in yourself when nobody else will. – Sugar Ray Robinson.

Concentrated thoughts produce desired results. – Zig Ziglar.

Read something positive every night and listen to something helpful every morning. – Tom Hopkins.

It is the mind that makes good or ill, that which makes us happy or sad; rich or poor. - Edmund Spencer.

Believe in yourself and you will be unstoppable. - Emily Guay.

People become really remarkable when they start thinking that they can do things. When they believe in themselves, they have the first secret of success. - Norman Vincent Peale.

If the mind of man can believe, the mind of man can achieve. - Napoleon Hill.

Add value to everyday. Sharpen your skills and your understanding.– Anonymous.

Creativity means believing you have greatness. – Dr. D. Wayne.

Start each day by affirming peaceful, contented, and happy attitudes and your days will tend to be pleasant and successful. - Norman Vincent Peale.

There is nothing training cannot do. Nothing is above its reach. It can turn bad morals to good morals; it can destroy bad principles and re-create good ones; it can lift man to angelship. – Mark Twain.

Always keep a window open in your mind for new ideas, people and situations. – Dolly Oberoi.

What lies behind us and what lies before us are tiny matters compared to what lies within us. – Ralph Waldo Emerson.

Faith is to believe what you do not yet see; the reward for this faith is to see what you believe. - St. Augustine.

Believe in a hope that a new hope is dawning ----- believe that your dreams will come true----- believe in the promise of brighter tomorrows ------begin by believing in you. – Anonymous.

Believe ---------and the magic will follow. – Spn.

Our intentions create our reality. - Dr. D. Wayne.

If you realized how powerful your thoughts are, you would never think another negative thought. - Peace Pilgrim.

The key to unlocking my potential is within me. It is the power of my thought, my vision, and my commitment, everything changes when you change. – Jim Rohn.

Man alone has the power to transfer his thoughts into physical reality; man alone can dream and make his dreams come true. - Napoleon Hill.

Commit yourself to the lifelong learning. The most valuable asset you will ever have is your mind and what you put into it. – Brian Tracy.

Wealth is the product of a man's ability to think. – Ayn Rand.

He who asks a question is a fool for five minutes. He who does not ask a question is a fool forever. – Mark Twain.

Continous learning is the minimum requirement for success in any field. – Denis Waitley.

Believing in you is an endless destination. Believing you have failed is the end of the journey. – Sarah Meredith.

Never underestimate the potential and power of human spirit. – Wilma Rudolph.

Nothing splendid has ever been achieved except by those who dared to believe that something inside them was superior to circumstances. – Bruce Barton.

Believing that you can is half the battle. – Sandra Gabriel.

Your thoughts become your words. Your words become your actions; your actions become your habits. Your habits become your character. Your character becomes your destiny. – Mahatma Gandhi.

The first step is to fill your life with positive faith that will help you through anything. The second step is to start where you are. – Norman Vincent Peale.

Minds are like parachutes - they only function when open. – Thomas Dewar

Attitude determines altitude. – Zig Ziglar.

Champions believe in themselves, even if no one else does. – Anonymous.

Our belief at the beginning of a doubtful undertaking is the one thing that assures the successful outcomes of any venture. - William James.

Intelligence without ambition is like a bird without wings. - C. Archie Danilson.

Learn something new every single day. You will never get old if you do. – Lois Bey.

You can do what you want to do, and sometimes you can do it even better than you thought you could. – Jimmy Carter.

Don't limit yourself. Many people limit themselves to what they think they can do. You can go as far as your mind lets you. What you believe, you can achieve! – Mary Kay Ash.

There isn't a person anywhere that isn't capable of doing more than he thinks he can. - Henry Ford.

Nothing is hopeless, we must hope for every thing. - Madeline L. Engle.

The uncommon man is merely the common man thinking and dreaming of success in larger terms and in more fruitful areas. – Melvin Powers.

The currents that determine our dreams and shape our lives, flow from the attitudes that we nurture everyday. – Anonymous.

The happiness of your life depends on the quality of your thoughts. – Marius Aurelius.

Most of us are just as happy as we make up our minds to be. – Abraham Lincoln.

It takes a single idea and a single action to move the world. – Anonymous.

Our destiny is shaped by our thoughts and our actions. We cannot direct the wind but we can adjust the sails. – Anon.

Optimism is essential to achievement and it is also the foundation of courage and true progress. - Lloyd Alexander.

To achieve the impossible, it is precisely the unthinkable that must be thought. - Tom Robbins.

Outstanding leaders go out of their way to boost the self esteem of their personnel; if people believe in themselves, it is amazing at what they can accomplish. – Sam Walton.

What a man thinks of himself is what determines, or rather indicates his fate. - Henry David Thoreau.

First thing every morning before you arise out of bed, say out loud three times, "I believe I can". – Anonymous.

Thoughts are like a flame, small thoughts produce small heat, big thoughts make an inferno. - Jim Lu.

To learn, you have to listen. To improve, you have to try. - Thomas Jefferson.

The philosophy of the rich versus the poor is this: The rich invest their money and spend what is left, the poor spend their money and invest what is left. - Jim Rohn.

Obviously, circumstances alone do not make us happy or unhappy. It is the way we react to circumstances that determines our feelings. – Dale Carnegie.

Change your brain; change your life. – Daniel O. Amen.

We ought to be more concerned about removing wrong thoughts from the mind than about removing tumors and abscesses from the body. - Dale Carragie.

To be wronged or robbed is nothing unless you continue to remember it. – Confucius.

I know with conviction beyond all doubt that the biggest problem you and I have to deal with – in fact, almost the only problem we have to deal with – is choosing the right thoughts. If we can do that, we will be on the high road to solving all our problems. – Dale Carnegie.

You are too blessed to be stressed. Stop focusing on the negatives. Embrace only the positives. – Dr. Bilal Philips.

We can't solve problems by using the same kind of thinking we used when we created them. – Albert Einstein.

The only way to discover the limits of the possible is to go beyond them into the impossible. – Arthur C. Clark.

All that a man achieved or failed to achieve is the direct result of his thought. – James Allen.

PERSEVERANCE, PERSISTENCE & TIME

Time, patience and perseverance will accomplish all things. Society may predict, but only I can determine my destiny. – Clair Oliver.

The habit of persistence is the habit of victory. – Herbert Kaufman.

We can do anything we want to if we stick to it long enough. – Helen Keller.

People of mediocre ability sometimes achieve outstanding success because they don't' know when to quit. Most men suceeed because they are determined to. – George E. Allen.

You have got to get up every morning with determination if you are going to go to bed with satisfaction. – George Horace Lorimer.

Sometimes a winner is just a dreamer that never gave up. – Michael Jordan.

Real leaders are ordinary people with extraordinary determination. – Lincoln.

Nothing can take the place of persistence: Talent will not; nothing is more common than unsuccessful men with talent, Genius will not; unrewarded genius is almost a proverb. Education will not; the world is full of educated derelicts. Persistence and determination alone are important. – Calvin Coolidge.

There will never be another now. I will make the most of today. There will never be another me. I will make the most of myself. – Robert H. Schuller.

The only good luck many great men ever had was being born with the ability and determination to overcome bad luck. – Channing Pollock.

Patience, persistence, and perspiration make an unbeatable combination for success. – Napoleon Hill.

I will persist until I succeed. Always I will take another step and if that is of no avail, I will take another, and yet another. In truth, one step at a time is not too difficult. I know that small attempts repeated will complete any undertaking. – Og Mandino.

Nothing great will ever be achieved without great men, and men are only great if they are determined to be so. – Charles de Gaulle.

A quitter never wins and a winner never quits. - Vince Lombardi.

Great works are performed not by strength, but perseverance. – Dr. Samuel Johnson.

The surest way not to fail is to be determined to succeed. – Richard Brinsley Sheridan.

 Some men give up their designs when they have almost reached their goal, while others obtain a victory by exerting at the last moment, more vigorous efforts than ever before. – Herodotus.

I do not think there is any other quality so essential to success of any kind as the quality of perseverance. It overcomes almost everything, even nature. – John D. Rockefeller.

If I had to select one quality and one personal characteristic that I regard as being most highly correlated with success, whatever the field, I would pick persistence and determination. The will to endure to the end, to get knocked down seventy times and get up off the floor saying "Here comes number seventy one". – Richard M. Devos.

Through perseverance, many people win success out of what seemed destined to be certain failure. – Benjamin Disraeli.

If you consistently and persistently do the things that other successful people do, nothing can stop you from being big success also. – Brian Tracy.

Keep going, for success lies just around the corner for those who refuse to quit. – Anonymous.

The majority of men meet with failure because of their lack of persistence in creating new plans to take the place of those that fail. – Napoleon Hill.

It takes the hammer of persistence to drive the nail of success. – John Mason.

It is the constant and determined effort that breaks down resistance and sweeps away all obstacles. – Claude M. Bristol.

The difference between the impossible and the possible lies in a man's determination. – Tommy Lasorda.

Victory belongs to the most persevering. – Napolean Bonaparte.

Continuous effort! Not strength or intelligence, is the key to unlocking your potential. – Winston Churchill.

When you get into a tight place and everything goes against you, until it seems as though you could not hang on a minute longer, it is then when you should never give up, for that is just the place and time when the tide will turn. – Harriet Beecher Stowe.

If you want to know your past, look into your present conditions. If you want to know your future, look into your present actions. – Padmasambhava.

Persistent people begin their success where others end in failure. – Edward Eggleston.

The future is purchased by what you do in the present. – Samuel Johnson.

The only way to excellence is to consistently improve yourself every single day. – Thomas J. Vilord.

A leader's job is to look into the future and see the organization not as it is, but as it can become. – Jack Welch.

Let me tell you the secret that led me to my goal; my strength lies solely in my tenacity. – Louis Pasteur.

The man who gives up accomplishes nothing and is only a hindrance. The man who does not give up can move mountains. – Ernest Hello.

Time is our most valuable asset, yet we tend to waste it, kill it, and spend it rather than invest it. – Jim Rohn.

If you don't think everyday is a great day, try going without one. – Jim Evans.

The past is over... forget it. The future holds hope....reach for it. - Charles R. Swindoll.

The greatest waste in all our earth which cannot be recycled or reclaimed is our waste of the time that God has given us each day. – Billy Graham.

I have fallen down before, but I am not on the ground now. If I fall down again, I will still rise again. – M.K.O. Abiola.

No one can keep you down unless you decide not to rise again. – John Mason.

To be defeated and yet not surrender that is victory. – Joseph Pilsudski.

MISCELLANY

Always give without remembering and always receive without forgetting. – Brian Tracy.

Always be mindful of the kindness and not the fault of others. – Buddha.

The secret of happiness is to count your blessings while others are adding up their troubles. – William Penn.

Stay committed to your decisions, but stay flexible in your approach. – Tom Robbins.

I can't believe that God put us on this earth just to be ordinary. – Lou Holtz.

Whoever is happy will make others happy. – Anne Frank.

We must all suffer one of two things: the pain of discipline or the pain of regret and disappointment. – Jim Rohn.

A man has two names: the one he is born with and the one that he makes for himself. – Aaliyah.

Man is not the creature of circumstances; circumstances are creatures of man. – Benjamin Disraeli.

Luck is when preparedness meets opportunity. – Earl Nightingale.

Men of genius are admired, men of wealth are envied, men of power are feared, but only men of character are trusted. – Zig Ziglar.

A habit is like a cable: we weave a thread of it everyday, and at last we cannot break it – so we must form good, positive, and productive habits. – Horace Mann.

You can get everything you want if you help enough others get what they want. – Zig Ziglar.

Your current conditions do not reflect your ultimate potential. – Anthony Robbins.

You don't just stumble into the future; you create your own future. – Roger Smith.

Opportunity does not knock; it presents itself when you beat down the door. – Kyle Chandler.

The more you seek security, the less of it you have. The more you seek opportunity, the more likely it will be that you will achieve the security you desire. – Brian Tracy.

We all have the gift of unlimited potential. – Anonymous.

If God shuts one door, He always opens another. – Woodrow Kroll.

Do not let the future be held hostage by the past. – Neal A. Maxwell.

Develop an attitude of gratitude, and give thanks for everything that happens to you, knowing that every step forward is a step toward achieving something bigger and better than our current situation. – Brian Tracy.

Once a man has made a commitment to a way of life, he puts the greatest strength in the world behind him. It's something we call heart power. Once a man has made this commitment, nothing will stop him short of success. – Vince Lombardi.

With each choice you make, you create your life. – Emily Guay.

Your income rarely exceeds your personal development. – Jim Rohn.

Your habits will determine your quality of life. – Denis Waitley .

In reading the lives of great men, I found that the first victory they won were over themselves.... self-discipline with all of them came first. – Harry S. Truman.

The man who says it cannot be done should not interrupt the man doing it. – George Bernard Shaw.

The individual who wants to reach the top in business must appreciate the mighty force of habit and must understand that practices are what create habits. We must be quick to break those old habits that break us and hasten to adopt those practices that will become the habits that will help us achieve the success we desire. – J. Paul Getty.

Self-discipline is the ability to make yourself do what you should do, when you should do it, whether you feel like it or not. – Elbert Hubbard.

The principle of competing is against yourself. It's about self-improvement, and being better than you were the day before. – Steve Young.

There is always, always, always something to be thankful for. –Stephanie Williams.

Wherever you are, be a good one. – Abraham Lincoln.

Today is the best preparation for what tomorrow may bring. –Julan.

We each build our own future. We are the architects of our own fortune. - Appius Caecus.

Small opportunities are often the beginning of great enterprises. – Demosthenes.

A wise man makes more opportunities than he finds. – Francis Bacon.

Happiness is not by chance, but by choice. – Jim Rohn.

Vision is the art of seeing things that are not yet visible. – Jonathan Swift.

The greatest happiness is to transform your feelings into actions. – Madame de Stael.

We make a living by what we get, but we make a life by what we give. – Winston Churchill.

What we do today, right now, will have an accumulated effect on all of our tomorrows. – Alexandra Stoddard.

A man can succeed at almost anything for which he has unlimited enthusiasm. - Charles Schwab.

Happiness doesn't depend on what we have, but it does depend on how we feel toward what we have. We can be happy with little and miserable with much. – William Dempster Hoard.

Motivation is what gets you started; habit is what keeps you going. – Jim Rohn.

Procrastination is the seed of self-destruction. – Mathew Burton.

There are those who see an opportunity, and those who SEIZE an opportunity. – Anonymous.

Let your dealing with others be of three types: if you can't <u>benefit</u> them, don't <u>harm</u> them; if you cannot make them <u>happy</u>, do not make them <u>sad</u>; and if you cannot speak <u>well</u> of them, do not speak <u>ill</u> of them. – Dalai Lama.

Speak in such a way that others love to listen to you. Listen in such a way that others love to speak to you. – Anonymous.

Be yourself no matter what. Some will love you and some will hate you. Life is not about pleasing everybody. – Maggie Rice.

Anyone who doesn't take truth seriously in small matters cannot be trusted in large ones either. – Albert Einstein.

There are seven sins in the world: wealth without work, pleasure without conscience, knowledge without character, commerce without morality, science without humanity, worship without sacrifice and politics without principle. – Mahatma Ghandi.

The way we dress has a remarkable impact on the people we meet and greatly affects the way they treat us. – T. Molloy.

Your wisdom and education can only be known by what you say. – Sirach.

The person who never changes his opinion never correct his mistakes. – John Mason.

No one makes greater mistakes than he who did nothing because he could only do little. – Edmund Burke.

Don't grieve. Anything you lose comes round in another form. – Rumi.

Don't' let your happiness depend on something you may lose. - C.S Lawis.

If plan 'A' fails, remember there are 25 more letters. – Chris Guilbegy.

Never regret. If it's good, it's wonderful ….. If it's bad, it's experience. – Victoria Holt.

www.ingramcontent.com/pod-product-compliance
Lightning Source LLC
Chambersburg PA
CBHW060943130726
48001CB00003B/1033